HOW TO THRIVE IN LIFE

An Essential Guide for Gen Zers

James Minter

Part of the

Eyes-Wide-Open Book Series

www.jamesminter.com

MINTER PUBLISHING LIMITED

Minter Publishing Limited (MPL)
3 Coach House Mews
Cheltenham, GL50 2AU

Copyright © James Minter 2025

James Minter has asserted his rights under the
Copyright, Design, and Patents Act, 1988
to be the author of this work

eBook ISBN: 978-1-910727-63-8

Paperback ISBN: 978-1-910727-62-1

Printed and bound in Great Britain by Ingram Spark,
Milton Keynes.

This book is sold subject to the condition that it shall not, by way of trade or otherwise, be lent, resold, hired out, or otherwise circulated in any form of binding or cover other than that in which it is published and without a similar condition, including this condition, being imposed on the subsequent purchaser.

CONTENTS

PREFACE iv

INTRODUCTION: THIS IS YOUR LIFE............................ 1

WHO ARE YOU, REALLY? 7

THE WORLD YOU LIVE IN 17

SETTING YOUR COMPASS DREAMS AND GOALS 27

BUILDING YOUR TOOLKIT SKILLS FOR LIFE................ 37

CONSISTENCY - THE SECRET INGREDIENT 47

PERSEVERANCE KEEP GOING WHEN IT'S TOUGH 57

RESILIENCE: BOUNCING BACK & GROWING STRONGER . 67

LIVING WITH PURPOSE AND INTEGRITY 77

STAYING HEALTHY MIND, BODY, & SPIRIT 89

LIFELONG CURIOSITY & GROWTH 101

CONCLUSION 109

READING LIST FOR LIFE'S BIGGEST QUESTIONS......... 113

BOOK REVIEW REQUEST 118

TITLES IN THE 'EYES-WIDE-OPEN' BOOK SERIES 119

ABOUT THE AUTHOR 123

SOCIAL MEDIA... 124

ACKNOWLEDGEMENTS... 125

COME TO THE EDGE

Come to the edge.
We might fall.
Come to the edge.
It's too high!
COME TO THE EDGE!
And they came,
and he pushed,
and they flew.

Christopher Logue 1968

The poem captures the moment of trust and courage as the figure pushes them off the edge, and they begin to fly, symbolising overcoming fear and taking a leap of faith.

PREFACE

A Gen Zer is a person born between 1997 and 2012, which means the age range of the cohort is 13 to 28 at the time of writing. If you're a **young teenager** (13–17), this book is your chance to peek ahead, to understand what life might bring as you get older. You'll find real stories, smart tips, and honest conversations about the challenges and opportunities waiting for you. Think of it as your guidebook for the road ahead.

For those of you aged 18 to 24 - stepping into adulthood, forging your path, and making big decisions - this book is written with you in mind. Here, you'll find practical advice, fresh perspectives, and tools to take control of your future in this rapidly changing world. Whether it's setting your goals, building resilience, or living with purpose, this is your companion for the next step forward.

And if you're towards the upper end of Gen Z (25–28), with some life experience already gained, you'll find plenty here to reflect on. Use these chapters to check in with yourself, refine your skills, and keep growing. Whether it's new ways to face challenges or ideas to sharpen your independence, there's always more to discover to keep thriving.

In an era marked by rapid technological change

and an abundance of information, thoughtful curation is essential for genuine understanding. Each book in this series has been developed through dedicated literature research, leveraging advanced tools such as Perplexity to ensure that every topic is presented with clarity, accuracy, and relevance.

The materials within these books are carefully structured to build a comprehensive learning journey. Throughout each chapter, you will find not only insightful content, but also practical exercises designed to reinforce your learning. This hands-on approach is especially tailored for Gen Z readers, empowering you to engage with concepts and apply them in real-world contexts in a deep and meaningful way.

Our goal is to inspire curiosity, foster critical thinking, and equip you with skills that matter now and in the future. By combining the best research with interactive learning, the Eyes-Wide-Open book series is designed to empower individuals to acquire knowledge and equip themselves with the tools necessary to make informed decisions about their future. We invite you to explore, question, and grow, keeping your eyes wide open to the possibilities ahead.

INTRODUCTION: THIS IS YOUR LIFE

Imagine for a moment that your life is a blank book, in which you're both the author and the main character. Each day, you write a new page, sometimes with excitement, sometimes with uncertainty, but always with the power to choose what comes next. This book aims to assist you in making those choices with confidence, courage, and kindness. Although you can't control everything that happens, you can determine how you respond, what you learn, and how you grow. This is your life. Let's make it extraordinary. Many people go through life without really thinking about where they want to go. Imagine trying to find your way around a new city using the wrong map, like using a map of Bristol when you're actually in Bath. You'd end up lost and frustrated! But when you have the right map, you can plan your route, make choices along the way, and even enjoy the adventure.

Why This Book? - You might be wondering: Why should I read a book about 'thriving in life' when everyone seems to have a different idea of what thriving actually means? The truth is that there isn't a single definition of thrive that fits everyone. Some people chase grades, others dream of fame, some want to help others, and some merely wish to be happy. What matters most is that you define success for yourself and live your life in a way that feels right to you.

As a young adult, you're standing at the brink of possibility. You have a vast world ahead of you, filled with choices, challenges, and opportunities. However, here's the reality: no one else can live your life for you. Not your parents, not your teachers, not your friends. They can offer advice, support, and love, but all significant or minor decisions are yours to make.

The Myth of the 'Endgame' - It's easy to believe that life is a race to some finish line: get the grades, get the job, get the house, and then… what? The reality is there's no final 'level' where you win at life. Life isn't a game you complete; it's a journey you travel every single day. Your goals and dreams will change as you grow, and that's not just normal; it's wonderful. The adventure is in the living, not merely in the arriving.

Living with Intention - Every day presents an opportunity to make choices that shape your future. Some days will be straightforward, while others will be challenging. However, the more you take ownership of your journey by understanding who you are, what you value, and what excites you, the more meaningful your life will become. Living with intention means not waiting for 'someday' to start pursuing your dreams or becoming the person you aspire to be. It involves making the most of today, even if it's just a small step forward.

The Value of Time - Here's a sobering and motivating truth: Life is precious, and none of us knows how much time we have. This isn't meant to scare you but to inspire you to make your days count. Looking back, you'll want to remember a life filled with curiosity, kindness, adventure, and growth, not one spent waiting for the 'right moment' that never came.

Always Have Something to Look Forward To - One secret to a happy life is always having something on the horizon, a project, a trip, a new skill to learn, or simply time with people you care about. When you fill your calendar with things that excite and inspire you, you keep your life vibrant and meaningful. Don't allow your dreams to gather dust. Keep planning, keep moving, keep living.

What This Book Offers - This book isn't about providing you with rigid rules or instructing you on how to live. Instead, it serves as a guide to help you discover what matters most to you, establish habits that support your growth, and develop the resilience to handle whatever life presents. You will find stories, exercises, and practical tools to assist you along the way.

Ultimately, the aim is straightforward: to assist you in living a life you can be proud of, a life that reflects your true self, filled with purpose and enriched by experiences. Your story is just beginning. Let's make it a remarkable one.

Ready to begin? Turn the page, and let's start your journey together.

Who Are You, Really?

Self-discovery and identity

1

WHO ARE YOU, REALLY?

The Adventure Begins Within

Before you can embark on your journey to succeed in life, it is essential to understand who you are. This may seem straightforward, but it is one of the most significant and at times, most challenging questions you'll ever encounter. The world is brimming with individuals telling you who you ought to be: parents, teachers, friends, celebrities, social media influencers, and even strangers. However, the only person who truly has the authority to decide who you are and who you wish to become is **you**.

Why Knowing Yourself Matters

Consider your life as a journey. If you're unaware of your starting point, it becomes challenging to discern which direction to take. Understanding yourself is like having a map and a compass; it enables you to make choices that align with your values, strengths, and aspirations. Furthermore, it prevents you from wasting time pursuing things that don't truly matter to you.

The Many Layers of 'You'

You're not merely one thing. You're a blend of your personality, your interests, your values, your strengths, your quirks, and your dreams. These layers make you unique. Let's examine each one in detail:

1. Personality

Are you outgoing or quiet? Do you like to plan things or go with the flow? Do you prefer spending time alone or being with others? There're no right or wrong answers, just your answers.

2. Interests

What do you love to do in your free time? What topics make you want to learn more? Your interests can point you toward hobbies, friendships, and even future careers.

3. Values

What matters most to you? Is it honesty, kindness, adventure, creativity, fairness, or something else? Your values are like your internal compass; they guide your decisions, big and small.

4. Strengths

What are you naturally good at? What do people compliment you on? Strengths aren't just about school subjects; they can be things like listening, making people laugh, solving problems, or staying calm under pressure.

5. Quirks

What makes you different from everyone else? Maybe you have a weird sense of humour, a love of collecting odd things, or a talent for remembering song lyrics. Your quirks are part of your charm; embrace them!

6. Dreams

What do you hope for in the future? Don't limit yourself to what seems possible right now. Let your imagination wander. Your dreams are the seeds of your future.

Exercises: Getting to Know Yourself

Ready to explore what you want for your future? Try these exercises to get to know yourself better. You can use the lined page at the end of the chapter, open a blank document, or just grab a notebook - whatever feels easiest for you!

Exercise 1: The Mirror Test

Write down five words that describe yourself. Ask a friend or family member to do the same about you. Compare the lists; what's similar? What's different? What surprises you?

Exercise 2: The "Perfect Day"

Imagine you're free of all constraints –
- What is your perfect day?
- Where are you?
- Who are you with?
- What are you doing?
- What does this tell you about what matters most to you?
- Why is it special?

Exercise 3: Strengths Inventory

List three things you feel you're good at. If you're not sure, take a moment to reflect:
- Have you ever helped someone else, or made a positive difference?
- Can you recall a time when you solved a problem or achieved something you felt proud of?

- Reflect on something you accomplished when you were younger. How did you make it happen?
- What resources did you have within yourself that compelled you to do these things?

Exercise 4: Values Check

Your values are the things that really matter to you. Below is a list of some common values. Choose the ones that feel most important to you or write down any others you think should be included.

- Honesty
- Kindness
- Creativity
- Adventure
- Loyalty
- Fairness
- Independence
- Learning
- Courage
- Trust

Now, pick your top three. Why did these three resonate most with you?

> When you understand what truly matters to you, you can use these values as a guide for decisions, big and small. This self-awareness helps you stay true to yourself, even when faced with peer pressure or uncertainty.
>
> **Exercise 5: Dream Big**
>
> Imagine your greatest dream, no matter how huge or unlikely it appears. What are you doing, or what experiences are you having? What makes these dreams so thrilling for you?

The Influence of Others

It's natural to be influenced by those around you, including your family, friends, teachers, as well as your religious or cultural beliefs, and even the media. Sometimes, their expectations can support your development. However, they can also make you feel like you need to conform to a mould that isn't right for you.

Become self-aware:

- Are you doing something because you want to or because you think you should?

- Whose approval are you seeking, and why?
- What would you do differently if you weren't worried about what others think about you?

Learning to listen to your internal voice while still considering and respecting others is a skill that takes time, but it's worth it.

Accepting Yourself

Everyone possesses strengths and weaknesses. Everyone makes mistakes. Part of knowing yourself is accepting yourself, flaws and all. You do not have to be perfect to deserve love, respect, and happiness. Your imperfections make you genuine and relatable.

If you ever feel like you don't measure up, remember that **no one has it all figured out**. Even the most confident individuals have doubts and fears. The secret is to continue learning, growing, and staying true to yourself. There're no failures, only experiences.

Your Story, Your Choice

As you progress through this book, you'll uncover more about who you are and who you aspire to be. You may find that you will change your mind along the way, and that's perfectly fine. Life is about discovery and growth.

So, who are you, really? Only you can answer that question. However, by exploring, reflecting, and being honest with yourself, you will begin to uncover the answer, and that is the first step towards a successful, fulfilling life.

Reflection: Where are you now?

Take a moment to check in with yourself. What has been on your mind lately? Are you feeling uncertain about the future - your career, studies, transitioning into a new phase of life, meeting new people, or simply trying to make sense of everything happening in the world?

It's okay if things feel overwhelming. Being honest with yourself about what's stressing you out is the first step in figuring out how to manage it. When you identify what's bothering you, it becomes easier to find ways to address it, and that's how you begin to take more control of your life.

Ready to take the next step? In the following chapter, we'll explore your world and how understanding your place within it can help you make the most of your journey.

The World You Live In
Understanding context and connection

2

THE WORLD YOU LIVE IN

Beyond Your Front Door

It's easy to view life as centred around your home, learning environment, workplace, or neighbourhood. However, the reality is that you are part of something much larger—a world of more than 8 billion people, each with their own stories, dreams, and struggles. Understanding the world you inhabit goes beyond geography or current affairs; it involves recognising yourself as a global citizen, connected to others in ways you might not always notice.

The Big Picture

Take a moment to picture the world as a large patchwork quilt. Each square is different, with various colours, designs, and textures, but together, they form something beautiful and complete. Your 'square' is unique, yet it's stitched to all the others. What happens in one part of the quilt can affect the whole.

You share this planet with individuals from every walk of life, various cultures, religions, languages, and backgrounds. Some reside in cities, others in villages; some have abundance, while others strive to get by. However, regardless of your origins or beliefs, everyone has the right to live their best life.

Empathy: Walking in Someone Else's Shoes

One of the most important skills you can develop is empathy, the ability to understand and share the feelings of others by stepping into their shoes and seeing things from their perspective. Empathy helps you connect, build friendships, and resolve conflicts. It also lets you see and appreciate the world through someone else's eyes, so you can understand their challenges and what they need to make them happy.

> **Exercise: The Empathy Experiment**
>
> - Think of someone you know who is different from you in some way: maybe they come from another country, follow a different religion, or have a unique feature or family situation.
> - Imagine what a typical day might be like for them. What challenges might they face? What might make them happy or worried?
> - If you feel comfortable, ask them about their experiences. Listen without judging or interrupting.
>
> You'll be amazed at how much you can learn and how much closer you'll feel to others, just by listening and hearing what they tell you about themselves.

Respect: Everyone Matters

Respect means recognising the value of every individual, even if you don't agree with them or understand their choices. It's about treating others the way you'd like to be treated. Respect helps us stay connected and build a stronger community within a world as diverse as ours.

Respect isn't just for people in authority or those who are similar to you. It's for everyone: classmates, teachers, shopkeepers, or strangers on the bus.

Disagreements are normal. What matters is how you handle them. You can stand up for your beliefs without putting others down.

The Power of Community

No one succeeds alone. We all need support, whether it's from family, friends, mentors, or even individuals we've never met. Being part of a community gives you a sense of belonging and purpose. It also entails a responsibility to assist others when you can.

> **Exercise: Mapping Your Communities**
> - List the different communities you belong to (family, school, sports team, online groups, neighbourhood, etc.).
>
> For each one, write down
> - what you give to that community and
> - what you receive from them.
>
> Consider ways to strengthen your connections and help others feel included.

The Ripple Effect: How Your Choices Matter

Every action you take, no matter how small, can impact others. This is called the 'ripple effect.' A kind word can brighten someone's day, while a careless comment can hurt. What you do and say makes a difference. For example, choosing to recycle, volunteer, or stand up for someone can inspire others to do the same.

You don't have to change the world overnight, but you can make a difference, starting right where you are.

Global Challenges, Local Action

The world faces significant challenges, including climate change, environmental degradation, poverty, and inequality. It's easy to feel powerless when confronted with such large issues. However, remember that every significant change begins with small actions. You can:

- Learn about issues that matter to you.
- Use your voice and speak up, write, create art, or share information.
- Volunteer or join campaigns.
- Support businesses and organisations that align with your values.

Seeing the World with Open Eyes

Travel, reading, and meeting new people are excellent means of broadening your horizons. If you can't travel far, explore your own community with an open mind. Try new foods, attend cultural events, or learn a few words in a different language. The more you experience, the more you'll grow.

Your Place in the World

You're unique yet connected to others. Your choices, attitudes, and actions matter, not just for your own life, but for the world around you. By understanding your place in the broader picture, you'll discover greater meaning in your journey and more opportunities to create a positive impact.

Reflection: Where are you now?

Do you ever feel the need to stay true to your values and find genuine, meaningful connections when faced with change? You're not alone. Many people your age feel isolated - even with constant notifications and digital 'connections,' it can still seem somewhat empty. It's understandable if you're craving something deeper and more authentic.

Staying true to yourself, rather than constantly comparing yourself to others, can boost your confidence in your own journey. Be kind to yourself - genuinely. Focus on your contributions and how you can use your energy and strengths to grow. Looking inward rather than outward can actually be the key to feeling more grounded and less overwhelmed. Concentrate on yourself, rather than focusing on how others are doing.

In the next chapter, we'll explore how to set your compass, discover your dreams and goals, and start charting your own course through life.

Setting Your Compass – Dreams and Goals
Vision and planning

3

SETTING YOUR COMPASS DREAMS AND GOALS

Why You Need a Compass

Imagine you're about to set off on a journey. You have a backpack, some supplies, and a map, but without a compass, you could wander in circles and never reach anywhere meaningful. In life, your goals and dreams serve as your compass. They give you direction, purpose, and a reason to keep moving forward, even when the path becomes challenging.

Dreams vs. Goals: What's the Difference?

Let's clarify a common misconception: dreams and goals are not the same thing, but they work together.

- **Dreams** are your big ideas, what you hope for, what excites you, what you imagine for your future. They might feel far away or even impossible.

- **Goals** are dreams with a plan. They're specific, actionable steps you can take to move closer to your dreams.

Think of your dream as the mountain you want to climb, and your goals as the steps you take to reach the summit.

Discovering What You Want

At times, it can be difficult to discern what you genuinely desire, particularly when those around you seem to have conflicting opinions. Here are some methods to begin uncovering your dreams:

1. Listen to Your Curiosity

What topics or activities make you lose track of time? What do you find yourself daydreaming about? Your curiosity is a powerful clue to your passions.

2. Notice What Inspires You

Who do you admire? What achievements or lifestyles make you think, "I'd love to do that"? Inspiration can help you imagine new possibilities for yourself.

3. Pay Attention to What Bothers You

Sometimes, what interests you is hidden in what frustrates you. If you notice a problem in the world that you wish you could fix, that might be a sign of something meaningful to you.

For example, suppose you're unsettled by the amount of food wasted by supermarkets and restaurants while reading about families struggling with food insecurity. In that case, you might feel a mix of frustration and determination. Instead of merely feeling powerless, you recognise that this irritation indicates something important: the need for a fairer, more sustainable approach to food distribution. This conviction sparks an idea: to create a platform that connects local shops and eateries with nearby charities, allowing surplus food to be redirected to those in need rather than being discarded.

4. Experiment and Explore

You don't have to have it all figured out. Try new things, join clubs, volunteer, take on small projects, or search out a book on the subject. Every experience teaches you something about yourself.

Turning Dreams into Goals

Once you have an idea of what excites you, it's time to turn those dreams into goals. Here's how:

1. Be Specific

Instead of "I want to be successful," try "I want to write a novel," or "I want to run a 5K," or "I want to learn to play the guitar."

2. Make It Measurable

How will you know when you've achieved your goal? Set clear milestones: "I'll finish the first draft of my novel by December," or "I'll practice guitar for 20 minutes every day."

3. Break It Down

Big goals can feel overwhelming. Break them into smaller steps. For example, if your dream is to become a doctor, your first goal might be to do well in science classes, then volunteer at a hospital, and then research medical schools.

4. Set a Timeframe

Deadlines help you stay focused. Decide when you want to achieve each step and write it down.

5. Stay Flexible

Life is unpredictable. If your interests change or you hit a roadblock, adjusting your goals is okay. The important thing is to keep moving forward.

Exercise: Dream Mapping

Dream Mapping is about letting your imagination run free to connect your hopes, goals and dreams.

1. **Write down three aspirations** you have for your life, making them big or small, realistic or wild – they're your dreams!
2. **Choose one** of them and break it down into three specific goals with clear milestones.
3. **For these goals**, write down the first step that you will need to take to start the process.
4. **Share your idea with someone you trust.**

> Discussing your goals makes them feel more tangible, and you may receive helpful advice or encouragement.

Staying Motivated

Setting goals is exciting, but staying motivated isn't always easy, especially when things move slowly or challenges come your way. Here are some tips and ideas to keep your compass pointing true and to help you stay on track and moving forward:

- **Visualise your success.** Imagine how you'll feel when you achieve your goal.
- **Celebrate small victories.** Every step forward is progress - recognise your achievements!
- **Find an accountability buddy.** Share your goals with a friend or mentor who can cheer you on and help you stay on track.
- **Remind yourself why you started.** When things get hard, reconnect with the dream that inspired you.

When Goals Change

It's normal for your dreams and goals to evolve as you grow. Don't be afraid to change direction if something no longer excites you or if you discover a new passion. Life is full of surprises, and flexibility is a strength.

The Adventure Begins

Setting your compass doesn't mean you have to know exactly where you'll end up. It means you're willing to start the journey, to dream big, and to take purposeful steps toward a life that excites and fulfils you.

Remember: your dreams are valid, your goals are achievable, and your journey is uniquely yours.

Reflection: Where are you now?

You might feel the desire to grow and improve, but it's not always easy to determine where you stand at this moment. Are you genuinely making headway, or just doing your best to get through each day? That's an entirely valid question. In a world where everything moves quickly, it can be difficult to know if you're progressing or simply staying afloat.

The truth is, even picking up this book puts you a step ahead of others because it means you're actively looking forward. And that's really important and matters.

The true secret? Growth doesn't have to be large or sudden. Small steps, done daily, begin to accumulate until they become part of who you are. Keep listening to yourself. Focus on what's happening inside, not just around you. That's where real change begins.

In the next chapter, we'll build your toolkit, exploring the essential skills and habits that'll help you achieve your goals.

4

BUILDING YOUR TOOLKIT SKILLS FOR LIFE

Why Skills Matter More Than Ever

Imagine you're embarking on a great adventure. You wouldn't set off without a backpack filled with useful tools - things to assist you in solving problems, finding your way, and making the most of every opportunity. Life is no different. The skills you cultivate now will aid you in navigating challenges, seizing opportunities, and building your desired future.

In a world that is changing faster than ever, learning how to learn and adapt is just as important as any single piece of knowledge. The good news? You can start building your toolkit today, regardless of where you are or what your goals are.

The Essential Skills

In today's fast-moving, tech-driven world, success isn't just about what you know; it's about the skills you bring to the table. Communication helps you connect, inspire, and make your ideas heard. Problem-solving gives you the power to tackle challenges with creativity and confidence. Emotional intelligence builds stronger relationships and keeps you grounded. Digital literacy lets you navigate the online world like a pro, spotting the real from the fake. And with adaptability, you can roll with the changes and turn them into opportunities. Together, these skills make you future-ready in a world that is constantly evolving.

1. Communication: The Power of Words

Expressing yourself clearly and listening to others is one of the most valuable skills you will ever possess. Effective communication enables you to build relationships, solve problems, and share your ideas with the world.

- **Practice active listening:** Give people your full attention, ask questions, and show you care about what they're saying.
- **Express yourself clearly:** Practice being clear and direct, whether you're writing an essay,

sending a text, or speaking in front of a group.
- **Non-verbal cues:** Remember that body language, facial expressions, and tone of voice matter just as much as words.

2. Problem-Solving: Turning Challenges into Opportunities

Life will throw you challenges, big and small. Problem-solving means staying calm, thinking things through, and finding creative solutions.

- **Break problems down:** Tackle one part at a time.
- **Brainstorm options:** Don't be afraid to think outside the box.
- **Ask for help:** Two (or more) heads are often better than one.

3. Emotional Intelligence: Understanding Yourself and Others

Emotional intelligence is about recognising your own feelings and the feelings of others. It helps you manage stress, build friendships, and make wise decisions.

- **Name your feelings:** Are you angry, sad, excited, or worried? Naming emotions helps you deal with them.
- **Empathise:** Try to see things from other people's perspectives.
- **Handle reactions:** Don't react immediately, but take a deep breath before replying, especially when feelings are intense.

4. Digital Literacy: Navigating the Online World

Technology is everywhere. Knowing how to use it wisely and safely is essential.

- **Be curious:** Learn how to find reliable information online.
- **Stay safe:** Protect your privacy, use strong passwords, and think before you share.
- **Balance:** Enjoy technology, but don't let it take over your life.

5. Time Management: Making the Most of Every Day

You can't add more hours to the day, but you can use your time well.

- **Prioritise:** Focus on what matters most.
- **Make a plan:** Use lists, calendars, or apps to keep track of tasks and deadlines.

- **Take breaks:** Rest is essential for your brain and body.

6. Adaptability: Embracing Change

Change is a part of life. Adaptability means staying open to new ideas, learning from mistakes, and bouncing back from setbacks.

- **Stay flexible:** Try a new approach if something doesn't work out.
- **See change as growth:** Every new experience teaches you something valuable.

How to Learn Anything

No one is born knowing how to do everything. The most successful people are lifelong learners. They remain curious and continue to grow, regardless of age or experience.

Tips for Learning:

- **Ask questions:** Don't be afraid to admit when you don't know something.
- **Practice, practice, practice:** Keep practising. Every expert or top performer got where they are by putting in the time and effort. The more you practice, the more your skills

grow, so stick with it and watch yourself improve!

- **Find a mentor:** Seek advice from people with experience. They can offer valuable insights and shortcuts to help you succeed.
- **Use mistakes as lessons:** Mistakes are opportunities to learn and grow. When you make a mistake, take the opportunity to learn from it and make the necessary adjustments. That's how you get stronger and smarter

The Role of Hobbies, Creativity, and Play

Life isn't just about work and study. Hobbies and creative activities help you relax, discover new talents, and connect with others. Whether it's music, sports, art, coding, gardening, or something else, make time for things that bring you joy.

- **Try new things:** You might surprise yourself with what you enjoy.
- **Share your interests:** Join clubs, groups, or online communities.
- **Let yourself play:** Play isn't just for little kids; it's a powerful way to learn and grow.

> **Exercise: What's in Your Toolkit?**
>
> 1. **List five skills you already have.** (They can be anything from 'good at making friends' to 'can fix a bike' or 'know how to cook.')
> 2. **List three skills you'd like to develop.** (For example, public speaking, coding, drawing, or managing stress.)
>
> **Choose one of the skills to focus on this month.** Find a way to practice it every week. Record your progress and celebrate your improvement!

Building Your Toolkit, One Day at a Time

You don't have to master every skill overnight. Building your toolkit is a lifelong process. The key is to stay curious, keep practising, and never stop learning.

Remember: every new skill you develop is a tool that will help you on your journey, opening doors for you, solving problems, and making life richer and more rewarding.

Reflection: Where are you now?

As you begin to understand who you are and what tools you need to develop, it can seem like there are so many options that it's hard to decide which way to go. Life moves quickly - before you've even had a chance to process one thing, something new is already in front of you.

Try to stay grounded in your instincts and what feels true to you. Choose a direction that feels right and move forward with confidence. Don't let the overwhelming number of options freeze you in place; too many choices can cause indecision and dissatisfaction. Take your time, explore what's available, then select a path. And if it doesn't feel quite right later, that's okay. You can always change course. What matters most is that you continue to progress in a direction that feels meaningful to you.

In the next chapter, we'll explore the power of consistency; how small, steady actions can lead to significant results over time.

Consistency – The Secret Ingredient
Habits and routines

5

CONSISTENCY - THE SECRET INGREDIENT

The Power of Small Steps

Picture this: you want to learn to play the guitar. You pick it up once, strum a few chords, and then put it down for a month. When you try again, it feels as though you're starting from scratch. Now, imagine you play for just ten minutes every day. After a month, you'll be amazed at how much you've improved. That's the magic of consistency.

Consistency is about doing something regularly, even when you don't feel like it or when progress appears slow. It's the secret ingredient behind every great achievement, whether it's learning a skill, building healthy habits, or achieving your biggest goals.

Why Consistency Matters

- **Builds Momentum:** Like pushing a snowball down a hill, small actions gather speed and power as they gather momentum.

- **Creates Habits:** The more you do something, the more automatic it becomes.

- **Beats Motivation:** Motivation comes and goes, but consistency keeps you moving forward even on tough days.

- **Leads to Mastery:** Every expert started as a beginner. Consistent practice is what sets them apart.

The Science of Habits

Your brain loves routines. When you repeat an action, your brain creates pathways that make it easier to do next time. This is why brushing your teeth or tying your shoelaces feels effortless; you've done it so many times, you don't even have to think about it.

The same principle applies to any habit you want to build, whether it's studying, exercising, reading, or being kind to others.

How to Build a New Habit

- **Start Small:** Choose something simple and manageable. Instead of "I'll read for an hour every night," try "I'll read one page before bed."

- **Pick a Trigger:** Link your new habit to something you already do. For example, "After I brush my teeth, I'll read one page."

- **Be Consistent:** Do it every day, even if it's just for a minute.

- **Track Your Progress:** Use a calendar, app, or journal to mark each day you stick with your habit.

- **Reward Yourself:** Celebrate your consistency, even with a small treat or a mental high-five.

Overcoming Common Challenges

"I Don't Have Time;" Everyone has the same 24 hours in a day. The key is to prioritise and fit small actions into your routine. Five minutes a day adds up to over 30 hours a year!

"I'm Not Seeing Results." Progress can be slow and invisible at first. Trust the process. Like planting a seed, you won't see growth immediately, but keep watering and caring for it, and results will come.

"I Messed Up; Now What?" Missing a day isn't a failure. It happens to everyone. The important thing is to get back on track as soon as you can. Consistency is about sticking to your goals most of the time, not being perfect.

Tools for Staying Consistent

- **Habit Trackers:** Use a notebook, app, or a wall calendar to mark your progress.

- **Accountability Buddies:** Share your goals with a friend or family member who can encourage you.

- **Reminders:** Set alarms, sticky notes, or digital notifications to prompt your new habit.

- **Visual Cues:** Keep what you need (like a book or guitar) in plain sight as a reminder.

Real-Life Examples

- **Athletes:** Olympic champions don't train only when they feel like it; they show up every day, rain or shine.

- **Writers:** Many bestselling authors write a set number of words daily, even when inspiration is low.

- **Students:** Top students review their notes regularly, not just before exams.

> ### Exercise: Your Consistency Challenge
>
> 1. **Select a small habit you'd like to cultivate.** It could be anything: drinking more water, exercising, journaling, or practising a skill.
> 2. **Commit to doing it daily for two weeks.**
> 3. **Track your progress.** Use a chart, app, or simply tick off each day in your diary.
> 4. **Reflect:** At the end of two weeks, notice how you feel. What's changed? What did you learn about yourself?

> 5. **Repeat for a further week:** It takes 21 days of consistent behaviour to form a habit.

The Compound Effect

Consistency is like compound interest in a bank account; small, regular deposits grow into something big over time. The choices you make every day, even the tiny ones, shape your future.

Remember: You don't have to be perfect. You have to keep going.

Reflection: Where are you now?

There's a lot of talk nowadays about mental health and wellbeing - and for good reason. Being honest about how we feel, both about ourselves and the world around us, is incredibly important.

Building good habits sounds like solid advice, but let's be honest, sticking to them isn't always easy. They say it takes 21 days to form a new habit if you stay consistent. But what do you do when motivation's low or you're just not in the mood?

That's where confidence plays a role. When we feel confident about ourselves, we make better choices and begin to see improved results. Sometimes, though, we need to really push ourselves—especially on difficult days—to stay focused on our goals. The more consistent we are, the more we adapt to change instead of resisting it. It's amazing how much easier life becomes when you adopt that mindset.

In the next chapter, we'll discuss perseverance: how to keep moving forward when life gets tough and why not giving up is the key to long-term success.

Perseverance – Keeping Going When It's Tough
Grit and determination

6

PERSEVERANCE
KEEP GOING WHEN IT'S TOUGH

The Road Isn't Always Smooth

Every journey, no matter how thrilling, has its rough stretches. You'll encounter days when things don't go your way, when you feel trapped, frustrated, or tempted to give in. Perhaps you fail a test for which you prepared diligently, get rejected for a role in the school play, or lose an important match. It's natural to feel disheartened. What really counts is what you choose to do next.

Perseverance involves sticking to your goals, even when times are tough. It's about showing up, trying again after setbacks, and not allowing challenges to deter you. You don't need to be a movie hero to be persistent; it's a skill anyone can cultivate and is one of the most effective ways to achieve genuine success.

Why Perseverance Matters

- **Success Takes Time:** Most achievements don't happen overnight. Behind every 'overnight success' story are years of hard work, failure, and persistence.
- **Mistakes Are Part of Learning:** Every mistake is a lesson in disguise. The people who succeed are the ones who learn, adapt, and keep moving forward.
- **Builds Confidence:** Each time you overcome an obstacle, you prove to yourself that you're capable. This confidence carries over into new challenges.

Famous Failures and Comebacks

History is packed with stories of people who sometimes failed spectacularly before succeeding.

- **J.K. Rowling** was rejected by twelve publishers before *Harry Potter* became a worldwide phenomenon.
- **Michael Jordan** was cut from his high school basketball team. He later said, "I have failed over and over and over again in my life. And that is why I succeed."

- **Thomas Edison** made thousands of unsuccessful attempts before inventing the lightbulb. He called each attempt a step closer to success.

Their stories show that setbacks don't have to be the end of your journey. They can be the beginning of something even better.

How to Build Perseverance

- **Setbacks Are Normal. Expect Them;** If you know that challenges are part of the process, you won't be so discouraged when they happen. Treat setbacks as signs you're pushing yourself to grow.
- **Break Big Goals into Smaller Steps;** When a goal feels overwhelming, divide it into smaller, manageable pieces and celebrate each small victory along the way.
- **Focus on What You Can Control;** You can't control everything, like other people's opinions or random bad luck. Focus on your effort, your attitude, and your willingness to try again.

- **Learn From Every Experience;** Ask yourself: "What went wrong?" "What can I do differently next time?" Every setback is an opportunity to become smarter and stronger.
- **Ask for Help;** Perseverance doesn't mean doing everything alone. Friends, colleagues, family, teachers, and mentors can offer support, advice, and encouragement when needed.
- **Keep Your 'Why' in Mind;** Remind yourself why you began this journey. Jot down your reasons for chasing your goal and revisit them whenever you feel like giving up - it can help you find your motivation again.

Difference Between Persistence & Stubbornness

Persistence is about moving forward with purpose, learning and adjusting as you progress. Stubbornness involves refusing to change course, even when it's evident that something isn't working. If you encounter a wall, don't simply keep banging your head against it. Step back, seek an alternative path, or ask for guidance. Flexibility is part of perseverance.

Handling Criticism and Disappointment

Not everyone understands or supports your dreams. Some people will criticise or doubt you. Use criticism as fuel for growth. Tell yourself that criticism is merely feedback. Ask if there's anything useful you can learn, and let go of the rest. Remember, you're living your life, not theirs.

Disappointment is tough, but it's not the end of the world. Allow yourself to feel it, then get back up and try again.

> **Exercise: Perseverance & Resilience in Action**
> 1. **Think about a time when something didn't go as planned, or you didn't succeed at something you tried.** How did it make you feel, and what did you do afterwards, even if it was just a small action you took next?
> 2. **From that experience, jot down one significant thing you learned.** This might relate to yourself and how you managed a challenging situation or reflect on what you could have done differently.
> 3. **Pick a current goal you're working on.** List three possible obstacles you might face and

> write down one way you could handle each one or what you could try if it comes up. This will help you be ready for any challenges you might face and keep you moving forward.

Real-Life Example

Imagine you're preparing for a major exam or business meeting. You study diligently and prepare, but your first attempt is less than you'd hoped. Rather than giving up, review your mistakes, seek assistance from your peers or lecturer, and adjust your plan accordingly. With each practice, you improve. On the day of the actual event, you're ready because you were prepared and didn't give up.

The Gift of Perseverance

Perseverance doesn't mean you never stumble; it means you keep going, no matter what. Each time you choose to carry on, you're strengthening your resilience, deepening your character, and growing in ways that will serve you throughout life, whether in school, at work, or in your relationships.

Remember, the journey to success is rarely a straight

line. It winds and dips, sometimes unexpectedly. But as long as you keep moving forward, step by step, you'll go further than you ever thought possible.

Reflection: Where are you now?

Take a moment to check in with yourself - no filters. How are you really feeling right now? Confident or a bit anxious? Grounded or a bit lost? It might be a good time to start thinking about small daily habits that can help you stay centred and live life on your own terms.

That could mean starting a journal where you jot down what's on your mind; something to revisit when things feel off. Or consider establishing a regular meditation practice to help you reconnect with yourself. If that's not your vibe, consider finding a mentor or an accountability buddy: someone who can support you and keep you on track.

Whatever you choose, just remember: your journey is yours alone. The choices you make don't need to look like anyone else's; they just have to feel right for you.

In the next chapter, we'll explore resilience, how to bounce back from challenges and grow stronger through adversity.

JAMES MINTER

Bouncing Back and Growing Stronger

Mental and emotional strength

7

RESILIENCE: BOUNCING BACK & GROWING STRONGER

What Is Resilience?

Imagine a rubber ball. When you drop it, it bounces back up. That's resilience in action; the ability to recover after being knocked down. In life, resilience means facing difficulties, setbacks, or even failures, and finding the strength to rise again. It's not about never feeling bad, angry, or frustrated. It's about not staying down for long.

Resilience is one of the most important qualities you can develop. It helps you deal with stress, adapt to change, and keep moving forward, even when things get tough.

Why Resilience Matters

- **Life Is Unpredictable:** No one's journey is smooth all the time. Whether it's losing a friend, struggling with a test, or dealing with family issues, unexpected challenges are a part of life that can affect anyone.
- **You can't Control Everything:** But you can control how you respond. Resilience gives you the power to choose your response, rather than just reacting to a situation.
- **It Builds Confidence:** Every time you bounce back, you prove to yourself that you're stronger than you thought.

The Building Blocks of Resilience

- **A Positive Mindset:** Resilient people see setbacks as temporary and specific, not permanent and personal. Instead of thinking, "I always mess up," they think, "That didn't work out, but I can try again."
- **Problem-Solving Skills:** When something goes wrong, resilient people look for solutions. Instead of simply giving up, they ask, "What can I do about this?"

- **Support Networks:** Friends, colleagues, family, teachers, and mentors can help you through tough times. Asking for help isn't a weakness; it's a smart way to get stronger.

- **Self-Care:** Taking care of your body and mind makes you better able to handle stress. This means getting enough sleep, eating well, exercising, and making time for things you enjoy.

- **Emotional Awareness:** Resilience doesn't mean ignoring your feelings. It means recognising them, understanding them, and finding healthy ways to cope.

Techniques for Building Resilience

- **Practice Optimism:** Try to find something positive in every situation, even if it's just a lesson learned. Optimism doesn't mean pretending everything is perfect; it means believing things can improve.

- **Reframe Challenges:** Instead of seeing problems as roadblocks, see them as opportunities to grow. Ask yourself, "What can I learn from this?" or "How can this make me stronger?"

- **Set Realistic Goals:** Break big challenges into smaller, manageable steps. Celebrate progress, no matter how small.

- **Develop Healthy Coping Strategies:** Find ways to deal with stress that work for you. This could be talking to someone, writing in a journal, going for a walk, listening to music, or practising mindfulness.

- **Stay Connected:** Don't isolate yourself when things get tough. Reach out to people who care about you. Sometimes just talking about what you're going through can make a huge difference.

Learning From Mistakes

Everyone makes mistakes. What matters is what you do next. Resilient people use mistakes as stepping stones, not stumbling blocks.

- **Reflect:** What happened? Why?
- **Learn:** What could you do differently next time?

- **Move Forward:** Forgive yourself and try again.

> **Exercise: Your Resilience Toolkit**
>
> 1. **Think of a time you faced a challenge or setback.** How did you respond? What helped you get through it?
> 2. **List three people you can turn to for support.** How could you reach out to them if you needed help?
> 3. **Write down three healthy ways you coped with any stress.** (E.g., exercise, talking to a friend, drawing, listening to music, meditating)
> 4. **Describe one thing you learned from this challenging experience.** How did it help you grow?

Real-Life Example

Imagine you've been looking forward to a significant event, like a sports final, a performance, or a holiday, and it gets cancelled at the last moment. You feel disappointed and angry. Instead of bottling it up or pretending it doesn't matter, you talk about how you feel. You decide to use the time that was freed up to try something new. Eventually, you realise you've discovered something new or met new people, all because you chose to bounce back.

Growing Stronger Through Adversity

Resilience doesn't mean you won't struggle; it means you'll emerge from the experience stronger, wiser, and more confident in your ability to tackle whatever life throws at you. Every challenge presents a chance to grow.

Remember, you're probably more resilient than you realise. With practice, support, and self-compassion, you can recover from anything and continue to progress toward your goals and dreams.

Reflection: Where are you now?

You've already begun making moves towards the future you desire; now might be an ideal moment to think even bigger. What else could aid your growth? Perhaps it's trying out a new creative hobby to see what ignites a spark in you. Or perhaps it's opening up and sharing your journey with friends or others you connect with, building a support network as you progress. The more you engage with others, the better you understand yourself, too.

So go ahead, explore, experiment, and stay curious.

There's a whole world of possibilities out there, and you've already developed the mindset to face it. With consistency, resilience, and a bit of grit, you've got everything you need to stay on course towards your dreams.

In the next chapter, we will explore how to live with purpose and integrity, making choices that reflect your values and help you build a life you can be proud of.

Living With Purpose and Integrity
Ethics, values, and meaning

8

LIVING WITH PURPOSE AND INTEGRITY

What Does It Mean to Live with Purpose?

Imagine waking each morning filled with excitement for the day ahead. Not because everything is perfect, but because you know your life has purpose. Living with intention means having a clear sense of direction and purpose. It's about understanding what matters most to you and allowing those priorities to guide your choices, whether big or small.

Purpose needn't signify a singular grand mission or career. It can be discovered in the way you treat others, the causes you champion, or the passions you pursue. When you live with purpose, even ordinary days can feel extraordinary.

Why Integrity Matters

Integrity is a term you may often encounter, but what does it truly signify? In simple terms, integrity involves doing the right thing, even when no one is observing you. It pertains to being honest, trustworthy, and true to one's values.

When you act with integrity, people know they can rely on you. More importantly, you can depend on yourself. You feel proud of who you are, and you cultivate a reputation that opens doors and attracts genuine friends.

Discovering Your Core Strengths

Core strengths are the qualities that come most naturally to you: the ways you think, feel, and act that allow you to succeed and feel like your best self. Knowing your strengths makes it easier to make choices you can confidently stand by and take pride in. When you're aware of your core strengths, you can become more empowered and optimistic about the life you're living.

> **Exercise: Your Core Strengths**
>
> 1. **What are the three things that people might often come to you for help** with (advice, cheering them up, solving problems)?
>
> 2. **When do you feel most like 'yourself'?** Think of a moment when you felt confident, engaged or proud of yourself. What were you doing?
>
> 3. **What did you do that made you feel strong,** energised or proud, even if it was challenging (help others, lead a group, stay calm under pressure)?

Making Choices That Align with Your Core Strengths

Every day brings decisions, some major, others minor. When those choices align with your core strengths, allowing you to use your natural talents and stay true to who you are, it becomes easier to choose the path that's right for you, even if it isn't the easiest or most popular.

Sometimes, doing the right thing means standing up for someone, admitting a mistake, or walking away from a situation that doesn't fit with who you really are. It takes courage, but it's always worth it.

- **Ask yourself:** 'Does this choice reflect who I am or who I want to be?'

- **Imagine the future:** 'Will I be proud of myself for making this decision tomorrow? Next year?'

- **Listen to your gut:** If something feels wrong, it probably is.

The Power of Kindness and Generosity

Living with purpose and integrity isn't just about what you do for yourself; it's also about what you do for others. Acts of kindness, big or small, can transform someone's day or even their life.

- **Smile at someone who looks lonely.**

- **Help a friend with homework.**

- **Volunteer for a cause you care about.**

- **Speak up if you see someone being treated unfairly.**

Generosity isn't just about money; it's about giving your time, your attention, and your care. The more you give, the richer your life becomes.

Building a Positive Legacy

Think about how you want to be remembered - not just in the distant future, but even tomorrow or next week. Your legacy is shaped by the choices you make each day. When you live with intention and integrity, you naturally encourage others to do the same.

> **Exercise: Your Legacy Statement**
>
> A **legacy statement** is a short description of the person you want to be and how you hope others will remember you. It's not about being perfect - it's about living in a way that reflects your values and leaves a positive impact.
>
> 1. **Write down a few thoughts about:** What would you like people to say about your character when they describe you (honest, courageous, loyal)?
> 2. **In what way** have your actions reflected who you are and what you care about, and how have you

> shown up for your friends, family, and community?
>
> 3. **When people look back on their time with you,** how would you like them to feel? What lasting impressions might you have left on people in your life?

Handling Peer Pressure and Difficult Situations

There will be occasions when you're tempted to follow the crowd, even if it doesn't feel right. Perhaps friends want you to join in on gossip, cheat on a test, or exclude someone from a group. In these moments, your values serve as your compass.

- **Pause and consider:** What would your best self do?

- **Say no with confidence:** You don't owe anyone an explanation for doing the right thing.

- **Find allies:** Surround yourself with like-minded people who respect your values.

It's not always easy to stand alone but is it always a more powerful position. (To be honest and authentic.).

Living Authentically

Living with purpose and integrity means being true to yourself and not pretending to be someone you're not just to fit in or please others. Authenticity attracts true friends, fosters self-respect, and leads to a happier, more fulfilling life.

- **Embrace your uniqueness:** Your quirks, passions, and dreams are what make you special.

- **Share your story:** Your honesty can inspire others to be themselves, too.

Real-Life Example

Imagine you're at a party when someone suggests doing something risky or unkind. You feel uncomfortable. Rather than going along with it, you choose to either speak up or quietly remove yourself from the situation. Later, a friend tells you they admired your courage. You realise that by remaining true to your values, you not only protected your integrity but you also inspired someone else to find their own courage

Purpose in Everyday Life

You don't have to wait for a big moment to live with purpose and integrity. Every day is full of opportunities in the way you treat your family, how you approach your studies or work and how you talk to yourself. The small choices you make may seem simple, but over time, they shape a life of purpose and meaning.

Reflection: Where are you now?

How do you feel now about the values you've chosen to live by? About the goals and dreams you've set for yourself. Have you found a routine or practice that helps you stay grounded and accountable? If so, that's fantastic - and if you're still figuring it out and just doing your best to stay motivated, that's completely valid too.

The key is self-acceptance rather than perfection. Embrace your strengths, make use of your resources, and don't be afraid to recognise the areas you still find challenging - that's where growth begins.

Take time to celebrate the small victories - those quiet, often overlooked moments of progress. Every step forward, no matter how small, is a sign of growth and effort. Don't underestimate how far you've come; even the tiniest steps add up over time. You're making more progress than you realise, and your effort matters more than you think. Keep going - even when it feels slow, even when it feels invisible. You're doing better than you know. Progress doesn't always announce itself with fanfare; sometimes it's quiet, steady, and hidden in the everyday effort. But it's there. Trust that every bit of energy you're putting in is building something for you. You're stronger, braver, and probably further along than you give yourself credit for.

In the next chapter, we shall explore how to maintain a healthy mind, body, and spirit, allowing you to continue living with energy, joy, and resilience.

Staying Healthy – Mind, Body, and Spirit
Holistic well-being

9

STAYING HEALTHY MIND, BODY, & SPIRIT

Why Health Matters

Success isn't solely about achievements, grades, or goals. It also involves feeling good, physically, mentally, and emotionally. When you're healthy in body, mind, and spirit, you possess more energy, focus, and resilience to enjoy life and tackle whatever comes your way.

Taking care of yourself isn't selfish - it's essential. Consider your health the foundation for everything you wish to do and become.

Looking After Your Body

1. Sleep: Your Superpower

Getting sufficient sleep is one of the best things you can do for yourself. Sleep aids your brain in processing information, enhances your mood, and allows your body time to grow and heal.

- **Aim for 8–10 hours a night.**

- **Maintain a routine:** Aim to go to bed before 11 pm or earlier and wake up at the same time every day.

- **Create a sleep-friendly environment:** Keep your room cool, dark, and quiet. Turn off screens at least 30 minutes before bed.

2. Nutrition: The Fuel for Life

What you eat affects how you feel and function. A balanced diet gives you the energy to think, move, and grow.

- **Eat a variety of foods:** Fruits, vegetables, whole grains, and proteins.

- **Stay hydrated:** Drink plenty of water throughout the day.

- **Limit junk food:** Sweets and processed snacks are okay sometimes, but don't let them crowd out healthier options. Avoid fizzy, sugary drinks.

3. Exercise: Move Your Body

Physical activity isn't just for athletes. Moving your body at least once every hour helps reduce stress, improve mood, and keep you strong and healthy.

- **Find activities you enjoy:** Walking, cycling, dancing, sports, yoga, anything that gets you moving counts, even doing household chores,

- **Aim for at least 30 minutes a day.**

- **Make it social:** Exercise with friends or family for extra fun and motivation.

Taking Care of Your Mind

1. Manage Stress

Everyone feels stressed sometimes. The key is to find healthy ways to manage stress and cope.

- **Take breaks:** Short pauses during study or work help your brain recharge.

- **Practice deep breathing:** Inhale slowly, hold, and exhale. Repeat a few times to calm your mind.

- **Talk it out:** Share your worries with someone you trust.

2. Mental Health Matters

Just like your body, your mind can get tired or unwell. It's okay to ask for help if you're feeling anxious, sad, or overwhelmed.

- **Reach out:** Talk to a friend, colleague, family member, teacher, or counsellor.

- **Practice self-compassion:** Be as kind to yourself as you'd be to a friend.

- **Limit negative self-talk:** Notice when you're being hard on yourself and try to reframe your thoughts. Negative self-talk will lead you to the very thing you're trying to avoid.

3. Keep Your Mind Active

Challenge your brain with activities that stimulate your thinking and learning.

- **Read books, solve puzzles, or learn a new skill.**
- **Stay curious:** Ask questions and explore new topics.

Nurturing Your Spirit

1. Find Meaning and Joy

Spiritual health isn't about religion, but rather about finding meaning, purpose, and joy in your life.

- **Spend time in nature:** Go for a walk, watch the sunset, or just sit outside and breathe.
- **Practice gratitude:** Each day, write down or think of three things you're thankful for.
- **Connect with something bigger:** This could be faith, meditation, art, music, or helping others.

2. Mindfulness and Reflection

Being present in the moment helps reduce stress and increases happiness.

- **Try mindfulness exercises:** Focus on your breath, notice your surroundings, or do a body scan.

- **Reflect on your day:** What went well? What could you do differently tomorrow?

3. Build Positive Relationships

Strong connections with others are essential for your well-being.

- **Make time for friends and family.**
- **Join clubs or groups that share your interests.**
- **Be open to meeting new people and learning from them.**

Balancing It All

You don't have to be perfect. Some days will be easier than others. The goal is to pay attention to your needs and make small, positive choices each day.

> **Exercise: Your Health Check-In**
>
> 1. **Body:** How are you feeling physically? Are you getting enough sleep, eating well, and moving your body?
> 2. **Mind:** How's your mood? Are you managing stress and challenging your brain?
> 3. **Spirit:** Do you feel connected, grateful, and inspired?
>
> Pick one area to focus on this week. Write down one simple action you can take to improve your well-being.

When to Ask for Help

Don't hesitate to reach out if you're struggling with physical, mental, or emotional issues. Everyone needs support at some point, and asking for help is a sign of strength, not weakness. There are people who care for you and are willing to help you.

Real-Life Example

Imagine you're feeling overwhelmed with work, or your job, or friendships. You begin skipping meals and staying up late. You notice that you're more tired, irritable, and anxious than usual. You decide to talk to a trusted person, start going to bed earlier, and take a daily walk. Gradually, you feel your energy and mood improve. Small changes can make a significant difference.

Healthy for Life

Caring for your mind, body, and spirit is an ongoing journey. The habits you build now will support you for years to come. Remember: you deserve to feel good and live life to the fullest, thriving in every part of your life and living fully with purpose and joy.

Reflection: Where are you now?

Now is a good time to check in and care for both your mind and body. Are you regularly moving your body? Getting enough sleep? Eating in a way that genuinely supports the kind of life you want? These are all choices you've made, and with consistency, they can really start to accumulate.

Take a moment to assess where you are right now. Is this the version of life you're happy with, or are there still dreams and goals you want to pursue? If there's more you're aiming for, that's okay. The next step is simply gaining clarity on what that looks like and how to move towards it.

You've already got what you need to build the life you want - the tools, the mindset, the experience. Now it's just about taking that next step. You've got this.

In the final chapter, we'll examine how to keep your adventure going, stay curious, make plans, and live each day with excitement and purpose.

The Adventure Continues – Lifelong Curiosity and Growth

Never stop exploring

10

LIFELONG CURIOSITY & GROWTH

The Journey Never Ends

You've reached the final chapter, but this is truly just the beginning. Life is an adventure, not a destination. No matter how much you learn or achieve, new experiences, challenges, and opportunities will always be ahead. The happiest and most successful individuals are those who never cease to grow, explore, and dream.

Why Curiosity Matters

Curiosity is the spark that keeps life interesting. It's what drives you to ask questions, try new things, and view the world with fresh eyes. When you're curious, you're continually learning about yourself, others, and the environment around you.

- **Curiosity leads to growth:** Every new skill, book, or conversation adds to your knowledge and abilities.

- **Curiosity opens doors:** It helps you discover passions, meet new people, and find unexpected opportunities.

- **Curiosity keeps you young:** No matter your age, a curious mind keeps life exciting and full of wonder.

Always Have Something to Look Forward To

One of the best ways to stay motivated and happy is always to have plans, goals, or dreams on the horizon. They don't have to be immense; sometimes, the small things make life special.

- **Plan adventures:** A day trip, a new hobby, or a project you want to start.

- **Set new goals:** What's something you'd like to achieve in the next month? The next year?

- **Celebrate milestones:** Take time to notice and enjoy your progress, no matter how small.

When you fill your calendar with things you're excited about, you keep your life vibrant and meaningful.

Embracing Change and Uncertainty

The world is constantly changing, and so are you. Sometimes change is exciting; other times, it can feel scary or uncertain. However, every change is an opportunity to learn and grow.

- **Be open to new experiences:** Say yes to opportunities, even if they're outside your comfort zone.

- **See setbacks as stepping stones:** Every challenge teaches you something valuable.

- **Trust yourself:** You've already overcome so much. You have what it takes to handle whatever comes next.

Keeping Your To-Do List Full

A whole life isn't about being busy just for the sake of it; it's about filling your days with things that truly matter to you. But don't mistake movement for achievement. Your to-do list can include:

- **Learning a new skill or language**
- **Volunteering for a cause you care about**
- **Writing, drawing, or making music**
- **Spending time with friends and family**
- **Exploring new places, near or far**
- **Taking care of your health and well-being**

When you look forward to what's next, you keep your sense of purpose and excitement alive.

The Power of Reflection

As you continue your journey, take time to look back and reflect on how far you've come.

- **What have you learned about yourself?**
- **What are you proud of?**
- **What do you want to try next?**

Reflection helps you appreciate your growth and guides your next steps.

Staying Inspired

Inspiration can come from anywhere: a book, a conversation, a walk in nature, or a new challenge. Surround yourself with people and experiences that uplift you and encourage you to continue growing.

- **Read widely and often.**

- **Connect with mentors and role models.**

- **Share your dreams with others, as you never know who might help you achieve them.**

Your Story Is Just Beginning

Remember: there's no 'end game' in life. The adventure continues as long as you keep learning, dreaming, and moving forward. You don't need all the answers; you just need the courage to take the next step.

Fill your diary with plans, your mind with curiosity, and your heart with hope. Keep your to-do list full and always have something to look forward to.

Reflection: Where are you now?

Lifelong curiosity and growth are transformative, especially in a constantly changing world. What you've gained from this book isn't just knowledge - it's fuel. Fuel to help you build a life that feels right for you, not one you feel stuck in.

Curiosity and growth aren't about working harder or doing more just for the sake of it. They're about becoming more - more connected to yourself, more fulfilled, and more in control of your own story.

You deserve a life that shows who you truly are. Remaining curious about yourself, others, and the world around you is one of the best ways to continue growing into the version of yourself you aspire to be.

The tools are already in your hands. You have the mindset, awareness, and experiences. Now, it's just about taking that next step — no matter how small. You're ready.

Thank you for beginning this journey. The world eagerly awaits your unique talents, ideas, and energy. Go forth, explore, and make your story truly remarkable. The adventure continues: enjoy every step!

Your Story, Your Legacy

Living a life you're proud of.

CONCLUSION

Your Story, Your Legacy

As you reach the end of this book, take a moment to reflect on the journey you have just experienced, not only through these pages but also through your own life thus far. You have explored what it means to know yourself, set goals, develop skills, persevere through challenges, bounce back from setbacks, live with integrity, care for your well-being, and maintain your sense of adventure.

But remember, this isn't the end. It's just one chapter in the incredible story that is your life.

You Are the Author

No one else can write your story for you. You possess the power to determine what matters, which dreams to pursue, and how to respond to the world around you. You might make mistakes, face setbacks, and at times feel lost, but you will also experience joy, growth, and moments that take your breath away.

Every day is a blank page. What will you write?

The Power of Small Choices

Success isn't solely defined by a moment or a single achievement. It is forged through the small decisions you make, day in and day out - choosing to be kind, trying again, learning something new, or standing up for your beliefs. These decisions shape both your character and your future.

Keep Growing, Keep Dreaming

The most important lesson is never to stop growing. Stay curious, keep learning, and be open to new experiences. Your dreams may change as you do, and that's okay. What matters is that you keep moving forward, always seeking out what excites and inspires you.

You Matter

You're special. The world needs your ideas, energy, kindness, and courage. Even when you feel small or unsure, remember that your actions not only affect yourself but also those around you and the world at large.

Your Legacy Starts Now

How do you want to be remembered? What kind of difference do you want to make? Your legacy isn't something you leave behind at the end of your life; it's something you create every day, with every choice you make.

> 'What you leave behind is not what is engraved in stone monuments, but what is woven into the lives of others.' — *Pericles*

Final Words of Encouragement

There will be challenges ahead, but you possess everything you need to face them: self-awareness, resilience, purpose, and the ability to continue learning and growing. Trust yourself. Be kind to yourself. Celebrate your progress, and don't hesitate to ask for help when necessary.

Above all, live fully. Fill your days with curiosity, compassion, and courage. Keep your to-do list full and your heart open. The adventure is yours; make it extraordinary.

Thank you for letting this book be part of your journey. Now, go out and write the next amazing chapter of your life.

The world is waiting for you. Your story matters. Make it a great one.

READING LIST FOR LIFE'S BIGGEST QUESTIONS

Here's a carefully curated reading list for Gen Zers interested in exploring the themes of this book: self-discovery, resilience, integrity, purpose, mental health, and lifelong growth. This list features both fiction and nonfiction, combining practical guides with inspiring stories.

Self-Discovery and Identity

- **Letters to a Young Poet** by Rainer Maria Rilke – Timeless advice on creativity, individuality, and finding your own path.

- **Siddhartha** by Hermann Hesse – A classic novel about spiritual self-discovery and the search for meaning.

- **The Alchemist** by Paulo Coelho – A fable about pursuing your dreams and listening to your heart.

- **The Perks of Being a Wallflower** by Stephen Chbosky – A coming-of-age novel that explores friendship, mental health, and acceptance.

- **Simon vs the Homo Sapiens Agenda** by Becky Albertalli – A heartfelt story about identity, courage, and being true to yourself.

Resilience, Perseverance, and Growth Mindset

- **Grit: The Power of Passion and Perseverance** by Angela Duckworth – Explores why persistence and passion matter more than talent for long-term success.

- **The Resilience Workbook for Teens** by Cheryl M. Bradshaw – Practical exercises and strategies to help teens bounce back from setbacks and build emotional strength.

- **Man's Search for Meaning** by Viktor Frankl – A powerful memoir about finding purpose and hope even in the darkest times.

- **The Compound Effect** by Darren Hardy – Shows how small, consistent actions add up to big changes over time.

Purpose, Motivation, and Goal-Setting

- **Drive: The Surprising Truth About What Motivates Us** by Daniel H. Pink – Explains the science of motivation and how to harness it for your own growth.

- **The Defining Decade** by Meg Jay – Why your twenties (and late teens) matter and how to make the most of them.

- **The Next Right Thing: A Simple, Soulful Practice for Making Life Decisions** by Emily P. Freeman – Practical advice for making choices with clarity and confidence.

Integrity, Ethics, and Living Authentically

- **The Ethics & Integrity Handbook for Teens: Tools for Successful Living** by L. Ron Hubbard – A practical guide to understanding right and wrong and living by your values.

- **All I Really Need to Know I Learned in Kindergarten** by Robert Fulghum – Simple, wise lessons for living a good life.

Mental Health, Self-Care, and Well-Being

- **Rhythms of Renewal: Trading Stress and Anxiety for a Life of Peace and Purpose** by Rebekah Lyons – Strategies for managing stress and finding balance.

- **Turtles All the Way Down** by John Green – A novel that honestly explores anxiety, OCD, and friendship.

- **The Sisterhood of the Travelling Pants** by Ann Brashares – A story of friendship, growth, and facing life's changes together.

How to Use This List

- Choose a mix of fiction and nonfiction for both inspiration and practical advice.

- Use workbooks and guides for hands-on exercises and self-reflection.

- Read novels for empathy, perspective, and understanding of diverse experiences.

- Discuss what you read with friends, family, or mentors to deepen your insights.

These books will help you explore who you are, build resilience, make wise choices, and approach life with curiosity and courage.

BOOK REVIEW REQUEST

If you found this book helpful, pay it forward by leaving a review of one or more of the following:

- **Goodreads.com, Your Reading Diary**
- **Amazon: The Literary Marketplace**
- **BookBub: The Book Lover's Hub**
- **Instagram: A Picture-Perfect Review**
- **Facebook Reader Groups: Join the Conversation**
- **Your Local Bookstores: Support Offline Communities**
- **Or email me your review so I can post it for you.**

Others who have not discovered this resource will appreciate it.

TITLES IN THE 'EYES-WIDE-OPEN' BOOK SERIES

Navigating the Digital Maze: Social Media, Technology & You

Step into the fast-paced world of digital life with this essential guide for Gen Z. Navigating the Digital Maze examines the influence of social media, technology, and online trends, offering practical strategies for building a healthy digital identity, managing screen time, and staying safe online. Featuring real-life stories, interactive challenges, and expert advice, this book empowers you to take charge of your digital world and flourish both online and offline.

Real Talk: Mental Health in a Connected World

Mental health matters now more than ever, and Real Talk is your go-to companion for navigating the pressures of modern life. Discover how to manage stress, build resilience, and foster genuine connections in an always-on society. Packed with relatable stories, actionable self-care tips, and stigma-busting exercises, this book helps you prioritise your wellbeing and support others on the journey to mental wellness.

Making It Work: Money, Careers & the New Economy

Prepare to take charge of your financial future with Making It Work. This practical guide demystifies money management, career choices, and the evolving world of work for Gen Z. From budgeting basics to side hustles and ethical investing, you'll discover the tools and inspiration to construct a secure, values-driven life, regardless of what the economy throws your way.

All of Us: Diversity, Inclusion & Finding Your Place

Celebrate what makes you unique and discover the power of community in All of Us. This book explores identity, empathy, and belonging in a diverse world, guiding you through the challenges of stereotypes, exclusion, and allyship. With interactive exercises and real-world stories, you will learn how to build inclusive spaces, advocate for others, and find your place in a changing society.

Voices of Change: Activism, Values & Building a Better World

Your voice matters, and Voices of Change demonstrates how to harness it. Immerse yourself in the realm of youth activism, from discovering your cause to constructing movements and making a significant impact. Investigate innovative strategies, ethical activism, and the resilience required to effect genuine change. Both inspiring and practical, this book serves as your guide to transforming values into action and shaping a brighter future.

Heart to Heart: Navigating Personal Relationships in Modern Times

Unlock the secrets to meaningful connections with Heart to Heart. Whether you're forming friendships, navigating romance, or establishing boundaries, this guide offers honest advice and interactive tools to support you at every stage of your relationship journey. Learn to communicate with confidence, resolve conflicts, and grow together in a world where relationships matter more than ever.

ABOUT THE AUTHOR

James is the father of two grown children, a stepfather to three others, and a grandfather to seven more. Therefore, he has a lot at stake. His only wish is for all children, teenagers, and adults to thrive in life, regardless of who they are or their beliefs and values.

He began writing fifteen years ago, creating books that appeal to the inner child in all adults and feature very British humour - **The Hole Trilogy**. He continued his creative journey by writing an eight-book series for children aged 7 to 9 years old - **The Billy Growing Up Series**. These stories are traditional, addressing negative behaviours with positive outcomes for children.

The **Eyes-Wide-Open Series** for Gen Zers grew out of his appreciation for the rapid changes affecting the world and his observation of how upcoming generations, like us all, are struggling to make sense of what's happening around them.

SOCIAL MEDIA
Websites

www.jamesminter.com

www.billygrowingup.com

E-mail:
james@jamesminter.com

X: @james_minter

Instagram:
instagram.com/james_minter_author/

Facebook
eyes-wide-open book series

ACKNOWLEDGEMENTS

Like all projects of this type, several indispensable individuals contribute to their completion. These include my wife, Maggie, who patiently endures my endless requests to read, comment on, and discuss my story. She also contributes editorially to the insights designed to support Gen Zers in becoming responsible adults through her role as a personal development coach. In addition, I am grateful to a circle of trusted friends and colleagues whose honest feedback, encouragement, and diverse perspectives have helped refine my ideas and ensure the content remains relevant and impactful for young readers. Their collective expertise, spanning digital literacy, mental health, and diversity, has been invaluable in shaping a resource that meets the real-world needs of Gen Z. Without their unwavering support and commitment, this project would not have achieved its current depth and clarity.

www.ingramcontent.com/pod-product-compliance
Lightning Source LLC
Chambersburg PA
CBHW011127070526
44584CB00028B/3807